The Viking Invaders

LOUISE SPILSBURY

raintree 🍃

a Capstone company — publishers for children

Raintree is an imprint of Capstone Global Library Limited, a company incorporated in England and Wales having its registered office at 264 Banbury Road, Oxford, OX2 7DY – Registered company number: 6695582

www.raintree.co.uk
myorders@raintree.co.uk

Originated by Capstone Global Library Ltd
Printed and bound in India

ISBN 978 1 4747 7778 0 (hardback)
ISBN 978 1 4747 7786 5 (paperback)

British Library Cataloguing in Publication Data
A full catalogue record for this book is available from the British Library.

Acknowledgements
We would like to thank the following for permission to reproduce photographs: Cover: Shuterstock: Nejron Photo: bottom; Mariusz Switulski: top; Inside: Flickr: Merryjack: p. 41br; Shutterstock: AnastasiaNess: p. 35br; Mats O Andersson: p. 43br; Catmando: pp. 10–11; Fotokvadrat: pp. 16–17; Givi585: pp. 22–23; Jpiks: p. 37b; Tomasz Kobiela: pp. 4–5; Vuk Kostic: p. 31r; Peter Lorimer: pp. 20–21; Lovelypeace: p. 39b; Zdenka Mlynarikova: pp. 40–41; Byelikova Oksana: pp. 14–15; OlegDoroshin: p. 11b; Prystai: p. 44; Alexander Schuessel: p. 13b; Alexey Seafarer: pp. 8–9; StockCube: p. 25b; Wikimedia Commons: pp. 24–25, 28–29; Christer Åhlin: p. 19r; Gunnar Creutz: p. 29b; Emil Doepler: pp. 30–31; Richard Doyle: p. 26; Eadfrith of Lindisfarne: p. 23br; Øyvind Holmstad: pp. 1, 5br; Olaus Magnus: p. 15r; August Malmström: pp. 34–35; Per Meistrup: p. 45; Richard Mortel: pp. 12–13; Nachosan: p. 21r; Thomas Ormston: p. 7r; Arthur Rackham: pp. 32–33; Eileen Sandá: pp. 38–39; Wofgang Sauber: p. 9r, 17r; Jakob Sigurdsson: p. 33r; Silar: pp. 18–19; The Man in Question: pp. 36–37; Kim Traynor: p. 27; Mark Voigt: pp. 6–7; Morris Meredith Williams: pp. 42–43.

MIDLOTHIAN LIBRARY SERVICE

Please return/renew this item by the last date shown. To
renew please give your borrower number. Renewal may
be made in person, online, or by post, e-mail or phone.
www.midlothian.gov.uk/library

Contents

CHAPTER 1

Age of the Viking

The Vikings were terrifying warriors who set sail from **Scandinavia**, an area in Northern Europe, to win fame and fortune. From AD 700 to 1100, they struck fear into the hearts of many people around the coasts of Europe and beyond.

The early Vikings were quiet, peaceful people who lived a simple life. They spent their days farming and fishing, making a living from the land and the cold seas around them.

The real horror stories about the Vikings began when they built ships that could carry them far from their coastal homes. They developed a taste for stealing treasure in spine-chilling raids and had no problem fighting and killing anyone who stood in their way.

The word "Viking" comes from the **Norse** word for a pirate raid.

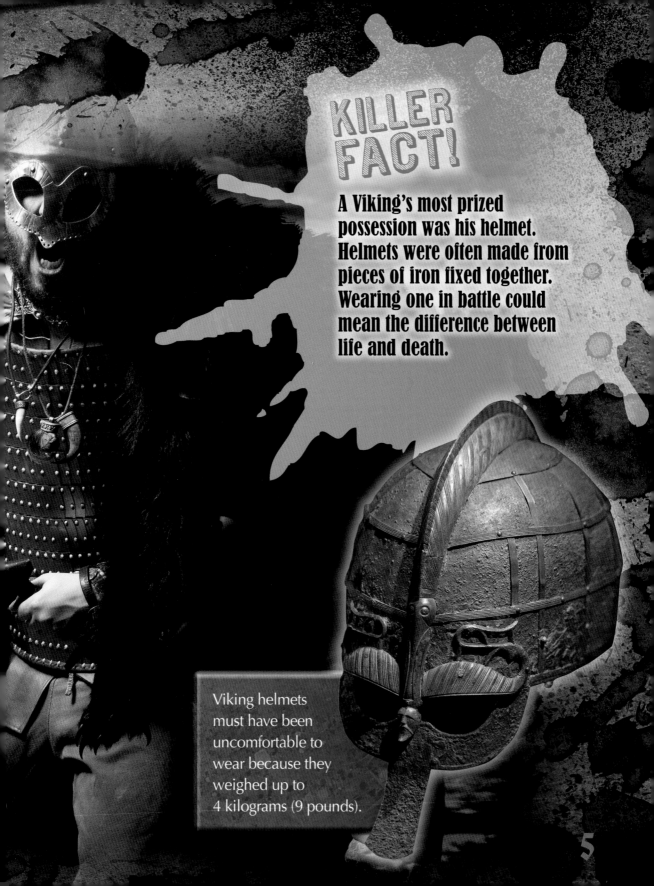

KILLER FACT!

A Viking's most prized possession was his helmet. Helmets were often made from pieces of iron fixed together. Wearing one in battle could mean the difference between life and death.

Viking helmets must have been uncomfortable to wear because they weighed up to 4 kilograms (9 pounds).

Hard lives

Given how horrible life was for Viking farmers in Scandinavia, it is not surprising that they started raiding foreign lands for treasure.

The long, dark winters in Scandinavia were cold and harsh, so farm animals such as cows had to be kept indoors. A Viking home was called a longhouse and it had just one room for all the family to share with its animals.

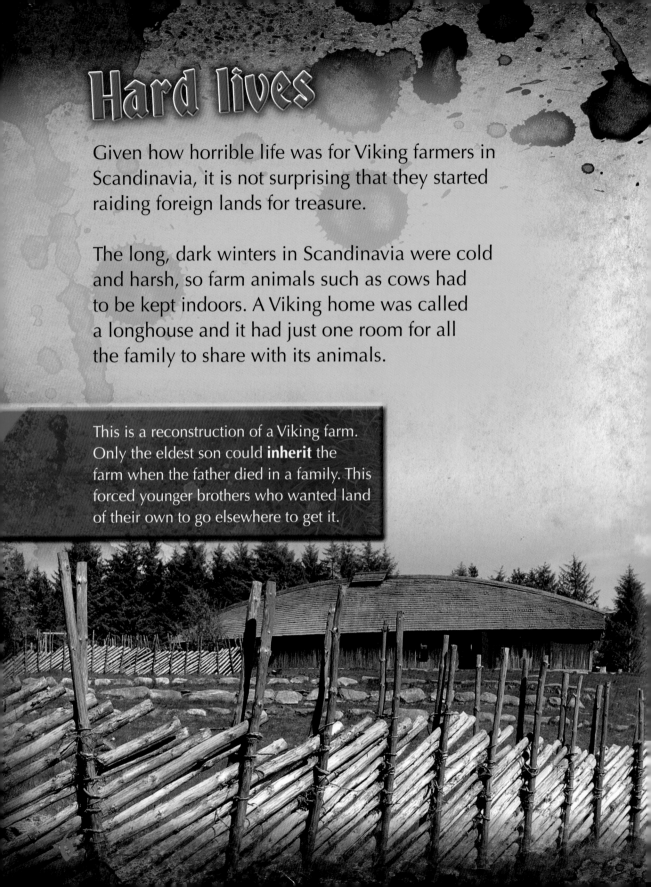

This is a reconstruction of a Viking farm. Only the eldest son could **inherit** the farm when the father died in a family. This forced younger brothers who wanted land of their own to go elsewhere to get it.

Farming on icy lands near the Arctic was difficult. Everything had to be done by hand, so life was tough and required constant hard work. Many Vikings left in search of better land to farm. Others left to fight and find treasure.

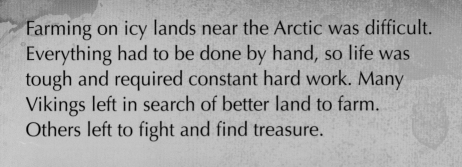

DEADLY DID YOU KNOW?

Viking boys were not only expected to work on the farm – they had to train as warriors, too. Viking boys were taught to fight using spears, swords and axes.

Viking longhouses did not have toilets. Families had to use a cesspit, which was a stinking hole outside the longhouse, dug especially for toilet waste.

Raids of glory

The first Viking raid took place in AD 793. After this proved successful, the Vikings started to send out vicious gangs of raiders to places far and wide.

Viking raids were violent and deadly. A gang of Vikings would arrive at a place by boat and attack the towns and villages along the coast or next to rivers. They stole treasures such as gold, jewels and coins. They killed anyone who tried to stop them.

Iona Abbey off the coast of Scotland was first attacked by Viking raiders in AD 795, and then again in 802, 806 and 825. At the raid in 806, the Vikings killed 68 **monks** from the abbey.

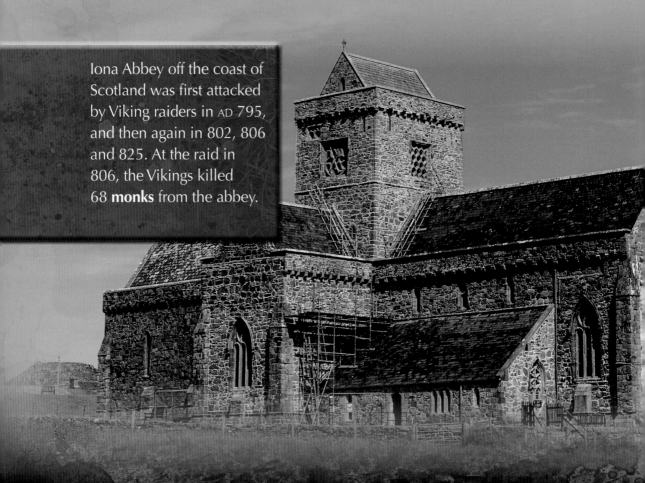

Vikings also kidnapped people on their raids and made them into **slaves**. They forced slaves to do the hardest, dirtiest jobs on their farms and in their villages. If a slave misbehaved, he or she was badly beaten. If a slave tried to run away, he or she could be brutally killed.

DEADLY DID YOU KNOW?
Most Vikings were mean and nasty to their slaves. They gave them insulting names such as Sluggard, Stumpy, Stinker and Lout.

Vikings kept their slaves in chains and heavy iron collars to stop them escaping.

CHAPTER 2

Lethal longships

The Vikings were masters of the sea because of their **lethal** longships. These strong ships carried them quickly and safely across stormy North Atlantic waves to attack unsuspecting people on coastlines far away.

Making longships was a tough, unpleasant job. Large wooden planks had to be cut, held in place and nailed by hand. Then, to make the ships watertight, workers had to fill in the spaces between the planks with animal hair mixed with tar and grease.

Longships had one large woollen sail and if the wind dropped, the Vikings had around fifty oars to keep up their speed. The rowers' hands became so blistered that the Vikings rubbed smelly fish oil on them to reduce **friction** and prevent painful chafing.

Longships were not only wide and stable, but also light and fast. These qualities made them lethal.

KILLER FACT!

At the front of most Viking longships was the shape of a creature, such as a horrific-looking dragon, carved in wood. When people saw the dragon on the front of an approaching Viking ship, they must have been scared.

Viking longships were often known as dragon ships because of their **menacing** dragon **figureheads**.

Open water ordeal

The Vikings brought terror to the lands they raided from the ships, but life on board was no picnic for them either.

At sea, the Vikings could not risk setting fire to their precious wooden boats, so their meals mostly consisted of cold and chewy dried fish or meat. They carried supplies of water, beer or sour milk to drink.

Longships had no covered areas, so Viking warriors mostly slept in the open on the hard, wooden deck, with only blankets or furs for shelter and warmth. Sometimes, they went ashore where they slept under woollen tents and lit fires to cook food and keep warm.

Viking longship sailors had to be tough. They faced huge waves and icy cold water.

KILLER FACT!

One particularly unpleasant Viking meal was fermented shark meat. This was created by urinating on dead fish, then burying it underground. Bacteria then got to work on the fish and made it rot.

Fermented shark meat is made from Greenland sharks, which are common in Scandinavian waters.

Stealth ships

Viking longships were not only made for speed and to survive high seas, but they were also designed for creeping up rivers to spring sudden violent raids on unsuspecting villagers.

These ships were very shallow so that they could travel in water only 1 metre (3 feet) deep. This meant they could be used to travel up rivers to **settlements** where people thought they were safe from attack by ship. They could also run straight onto a beach or up a shallow riverbank.

Longships were very light for their size. They had parts that could be temporarily removed so the Vikings could drag the ships overland to get to a nearby river without having to sail out to sea again.

Sleek Viking ships could be quickly hauled out of the water and onto land during a raid.

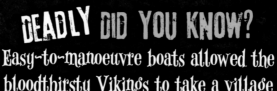

DEADLY DID YOU KNOW?

Easy-to-manoeuvre boats allowed the bloodthirsty Vikings to take a village by surprise and jump out and start their attack before their victims had time to prepare defences.

The Vikings were able to travel across large distances, moving from river to river, by carrying and dragging their boats overland.

CHAPTER 3

Weapons of war

One reason the Vikings proved so deadly and their raids so hard to resist was the murderous weapons they used and the savagery with which they used them.

The Viking spear was an iron blade on a wooden pole and was up to 3 metres (9 feet) long. The Vikings could throw two spears at a time using both hands, or even catch an enemy spear as it flew towards them, and throw it back with deadly accuracy.

Viking axes were lethal. They had wide, curved blades or blades shaped like sharp spikes, and long handles. They were used to cut enemies with heavy blows and were also thrown. A warrior with a large axe would often take cover behind the front line of a gang of Vikings and then rush out to attack **opponents** when he was close enough.

A Viking warrior charging forward wielding an axe must have been a terrifying sight for any opponent.

Viking shields were hooked onto the sides of a longship. When the ship pulled up onto land, the warriors could grab them quickly and jump out to begin their deadly attack.

Strong, circular shields were made of wood and iron and were up to 1 metre (3 feet) wide.

Lethal blades

A Viking's most prized weapon was his sword. Swords were usually the most expensive item that a Viking owned. They were also the most lethal and efficient of all the Viking weapons.

Swords were strong but also light and able to bend. This meant that the Vikings could hold them in one hand while in the other hand they held a shield. Sword handles were often made of bone, **antlers** or precious metals such as gold and silver.

These swords could be 1 metre (3 feet) long and were usually double-edged. Both edges of the blade were very sharp and equally dangerous. A warrior carried his sword in a leather holder hanging from his waist, so he could pull it out quickly in a fight.

Viking fights were brutal, ferocious affairs with swords crashing loudly against shields.

DEADLY DID YOU KNOW?
Viking swords were so deadly that the Vikings often gave them bloodcurdling names, such as Viper, Gnawer, Flame of Battle, Hole-Maker and Leg-Biter.

Viking steel swords were less likely to break and lose their sharpness in battle than their victims' iron ones.

Going berserk

Viking leaders wore long tunics of iron **chain mail** to protect themselves from enemy weapons. Most Vikings wore padded leather shirts to absorb the impact of arrow or sword strikes.

Warriors called berserkers were the most terrifying of all. These vikings wore bearskins, believing that this would give them the strength and terror of a bear. Berserkers believed they did not need to wear battle armour because Odin, the Viking god of war, gave them superpowers.

The berserkers sometimes formed gangs that fought in the same bloodthirsty way, without fear for their own life and ignoring the pain of wounds. They would work themselves into a frenzy so intense it is said they howled like wild animals and bit on the edges of their shields out of pure rage.

It took a lot of strength to fight while wearing a heavy helmet and a tunic of iron chain mail.

KILLER FACT!

The word "beserk", which means "out of control", comes from the Viking word for the fierce warriors called berserkers, who fought with an uncontrollable fury.

The berserkers are among the most feared of all Vikings. This Viking chess piece shows a wild-eyed berserker biting his shield.

CHAPTER 4

Deadly attack forces

The Vikings made hit-and-run raids on cities and towns along any coasts they could reach by ship. Their deadly attacks spread fear like wildfire across Europe.

The Vikings first raided England in AD 793. During this raid they attacked a **monastery** in northern England called Lindisfarne. The monks living there had no weapons and they did not even try to fight back. The Vikings burned down their buildings, chased the monks into the sea to drown and stole their treasure.

Vikings destroyed the monastery at Lindisfarne. Monasteries were easy targets for the Vikings because they had no defences and the monks did not fight back.

On most of their raids, Vikings crash-landed their ships at dawn to launch a surprise attack. Having their ships nearby meant that the Vikings could quickly stash all the treasures that they stole, then climb back on board for a swift getaway.

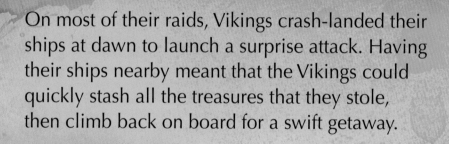

DEADLY DID YOU KNOW?

During raids, the Vikings would leap from boats, scream battle cries and storm through buildings. They murdered villagers while they were still asleep in their beds.

Valuable **manuscripts** were stolen from the monasteries.

Spreading terror

A gang of vicious Vikings carrying deadly weapons and screaming threats must have been a terrifying sight. The Vikings travelled far and wide to burn, **plunder** and kill with ever bigger forces.

At one time, 120 boats carrying up to four thousand Viking warriors sailed up the River Seine to attack Paris, France. They were met by two French forces. They finished off one quickly. They took more than one hundred prisoners and hanged them on the riverbank to frighten off the remaining opponents.

After the Vikings had defeated the French, they demanded treasure. The French king was so terrified of the Viking warriors that he handed over a fortune in gold and silver to make them go away.

KILLER FACT!

To make themselves look even scarier, Viking raiders filed their teeth into sharp points or cut grooves into them. They also rubbed red berry juice onto teeth so that they looked more bloodthirsty.

The Vikings set fire to buildings during raids to strike even more terror into the hearts of opponents.

Total war

After years of spreading terror, stealing treasures and kidnapping slaves, the Vikings decided not only to raid places, but also to **conquer** them.

In AD 865, the Vikings gathered a great army and set out on ships to wage total war on **Anglo-Saxon** kingdoms. They fought fierce battles at sea and destroyed lands. They murdered many people, and soon the Vikings had conquered most of England.

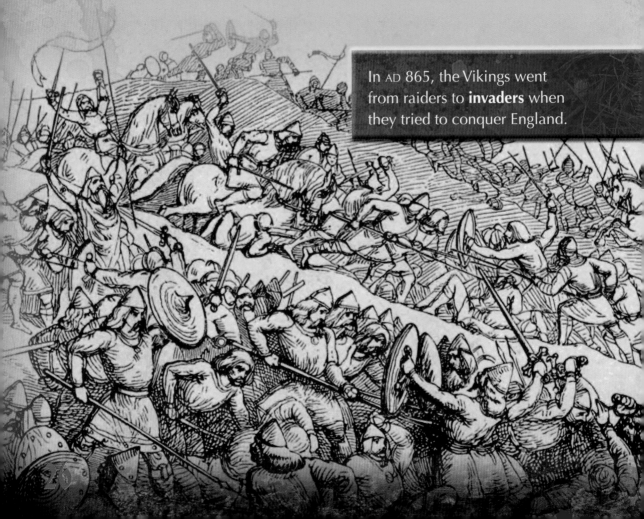

In AD 865, the Vikings went from raiders to **invaders** when they tried to conquer England.

Vicious battles were fought between Viking armies that roamed the countryside and English defenders. Hundreds of people were brutally killed and fields were stained with blood. Eventually, most areas were brought back under English control, but not before the Vikings had established several of their own cities and settlements.

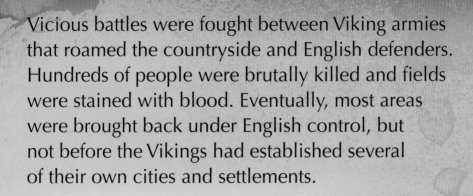

DEADLY DID YOU KNOW?
There is evidence that fierce female Vikings fought alongside men. Female Viking warriors were known as shieldmaidens. Bodies of badly injured female fighters have been found beside male Vikings in warrior graves.

These remains were discovered in a **mass grave** of dead Vikings from the great army found in England.

27

CHAPTER 5

Gruesome gods

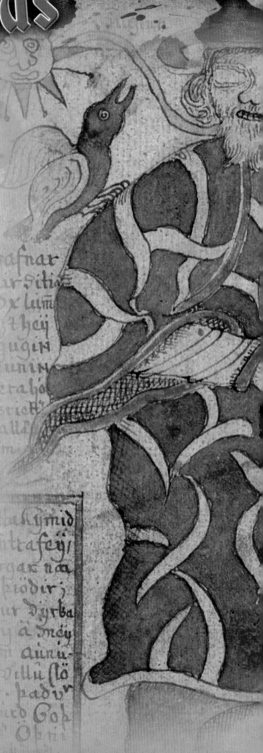

Belief in their gruesome gods and goddesses gave Vikings courage in their bloody battles and raids. They believed dying in battle would bring them to a glorious **afterlife**.

Thor was the powerful god of thunder. The Vikings believed that a flash of lightning meant Thor had flung his hammer, which he used to overcome all evil and misbehaving giants.

Odin was the one-eyed god of war and king of the gods. Warriors who died in battle went to live with him. He carried a spear and rode an eight-legged horse. Odin had two ravens called Thought and Memory. These black birds flew around the world in the day and at night, and told Odin all that they had seen.

Odin's ravens were also considered to be omens (signs) of death.

KILLER FACT!

Viking lives were full of danger, so many Vikings wore lucky charms called amulets. They believed wearing an amulet in the shape of Thor's hammer would mean Thor would protect them from evil.

Thor's hammer was a powerful amulet in Viking times.

Terrifying worlds

Vikings believed that the world was made up of nine different realms (worlds). Some of these worlds were ruled over and **inhabited** by terrifying gods, giants, dwarfs and elves.

Vikings gods lived in a kingdom called Asgard. The Earth where humans lived was known as Midgard. Midgard was connected to Asgard by a rainbow bridge. Giants lived in an underworld and were the arch-enemies of the gods.

The gods were there to fight the giants and other evil forces. The Vikings believed that the world would end with one dreadful, final battle known as Ragnarök, between the gods and the giants. This struck fear into Viking hearts.

The Vikings believed that another of the nine worlds, Muspelheim, was a burning-hot place. It was home to terrible fire giants and fire demons and was filled with lava and flames.

Vikings believed that the evil fire giant Surt, who guarded the world of Muspelheim, would one day set fire to Asgard.

This is an illustration of the world in which the Vikings believed fire demons and giants lived.

Hall of the slain

The hall of the slain, known as Valhalla, was where Vikings believed the bravest warriors went after they died. Valhalla was a great hall in Asgard ruled over by the god Odin.

Valhalla was a strange kind of heaven. Vikings believed that during the day, dead warriors left Valhalla to fight viciously against each other. This was to keep them fighting fit and ready for the final battle between gods and giants.

After the fighting, the wounded warriors would be magically healed. Any warriors who had died (again) in these scary battles would come to life again. Then they would return to Valhalla to spend the nights feasting and drinking.

In Valhalla, great female warriors known as Valkyries decided what would happen to dead warriors.

KILLER FACT!

Criminals who died faced a horrible afterlife. They went to a realm of darkness ruled over by the goddess Hel. Here they were tormented by a blood-sucking dragon and a castle filled with poisonous serpents.

Vikings believed a magical female goat called Heidrun sat on the roof of Valhalla producing mead, which was an alcoholic drink, for the dead warriors to drink.

33

CHAPTER 6

Death cult

Death was a part of life for the Vikings. They faced death on raids and in battles and their large religious celebrations were often centred on death or **sacrifice**.

The Vikings believed that it was important to keep their gods happy. To do this, they made regular sacrifices. Vikings believed that in return for a sacrifice, the gods would make sure they got something they wanted such as good weather or wealth.

A feast and sacrifice could be dedicated to any of the gods. These festivals were sacred and important, but also like parties.

A sacrifice usually took place during a feast or ceremony. Animals such as pigs and horses were often sacrificed. The meat was boiled in large cooking pits. Vikings believed blood from sacrifices had special powers, so they sprinkled it on statues of the gods and themselves.

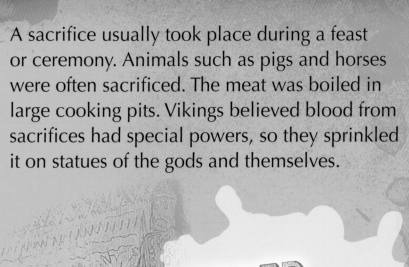

KILLER FACT!

Vikings greatly respected horses. They believed horses could bring good luck, so the animals were often sacrificed in a ceremony to have a good harvest or a successful raid.

Vikings sacrificed horses to honour the gods, and then ate the horse meat at a feast.

Human sacrifice

For some gods, an animal sacrifice was not good enough. Vikings believed that the god Odin would be satisfied only when humans were also put to death in his honour.

Some humans were sacrificed to the gods at religious festivals. These sacrifices took place in special buildings or outside in natural spaces that had been specially prepared for the ritual. At these ceremonies, prisoners of war were often sacrificed.

Vikings believed a human life was the most valuable sacrifice that they could make to the gods.

The poor victims of these sacrifices were killed in different ways. Some were strangled. Others were hit on the head or had their throat slit. Others were hanged from the trees – dead bodies were found by archaeologists with the noose still around their neck.

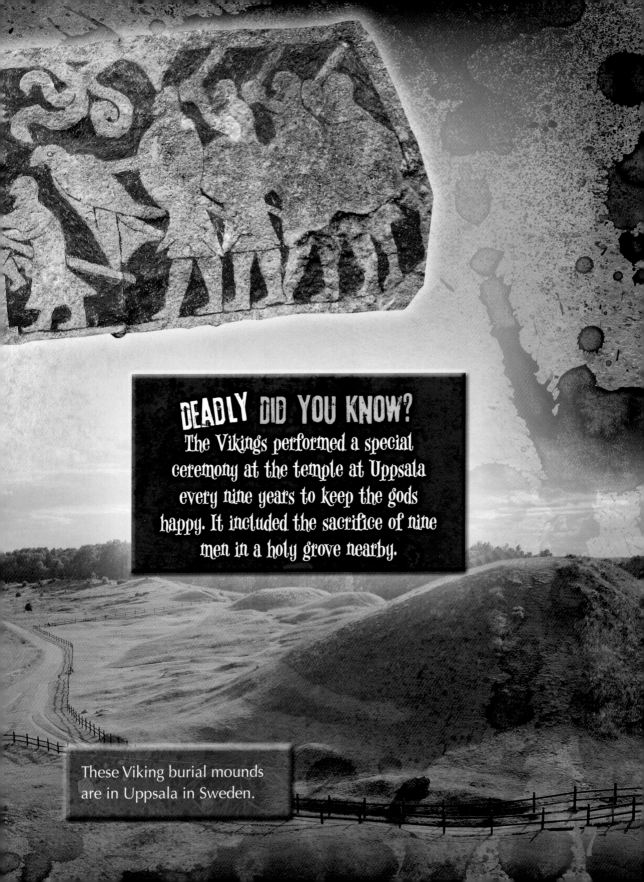

DEADLY DID YOU KNOW?
The Vikings performed a special ceremony at the temple at Uppsala every nine years to keep the gods happy. It included the sacrifice of nine men in a holy grove nearby.

These Viking burial mounds are in Uppsala in Sweden.

Gruesome graves

Vikings were buried with all the belongings that they would need in the afterlife. A warrior's most highly prized weapons were buried with him and so were his unfortunate slaves.

The wealthiest Vikings were buried in ships. Viking men had tools, clothing, weapons and even money buried with them. Most Viking women spent their lives at home or on their farm, so they were buried with items such as jewellery, bowls, knives and cooking pots.

After a Viking was buried, piles of stone and soil were usually laid on top of the body.

Viking slaves were sometimes sacrificed when their masters died. They were often **beheaded** before being placed in the grave to be useful to their owner in the afterlife. A number of Viking warrior graves have been found to contain the remains of slaves.

KILLER FACT!

The Oseberg was a Viking burial ship in which the bodies of two women were found. One was someone important, perhaps a queen, and the other woman was probably her slave.

Inside the Oseberg ship there were also the bones of fourteen or fifteen horses, a cat, birds, a bull, a cow and four dogs.

Burning burials

Not all dead Vikings were buried in graves in the ground. Many were burned on a large, very hot fire, called a funeral pyre. Flames from these funeral pyres could be seen far and wide.

Most funeral fires were on land. The body was dressed in fine clothes. Gifts and belongings were laid beside it on a pile of wooden logs, up to 20 metres (65 feet) high. Animals, and sometimes people, were sacrificed and placed there, too. Then the fire was lit.

For the Vikings, boats were a symbol of safe passage into the afterlife. Sometimes, an important leader would be placed on his ship, which was then set alight. As it burned, it drifted out to sea as people watched on from the shore.

Viking funeral pyres were huge and a vast amount of wood was used to ensure the blaze burned brightly.

KILLER FACT!

After a funeral fire, people sifted through the ash and buried the remains of the body and the belongings, usually in an urn.

This is a Viking urn. Urns are containers that hold the ashes of people whose bodies have been cremated (burned).

Horrendous heroes

Viking warriors risked their lives so fearlessly in battle because they believed their time of death was preordained (already chosen). With nothing to lose, some Vikings became famous for their horrendous lives and even worse deaths!

Ragnar Lodbrok was a legendary Viking raider. He led many of the brutal attacks on Paris, and other parts of France, as well as England. Lodbrok's nickname was Shaggy Breeches because he wore trousers of animal fur. His success as a warrior made him a powerful lord. He is said to have been killed when a king threw him into a pit of poisonous snakes.

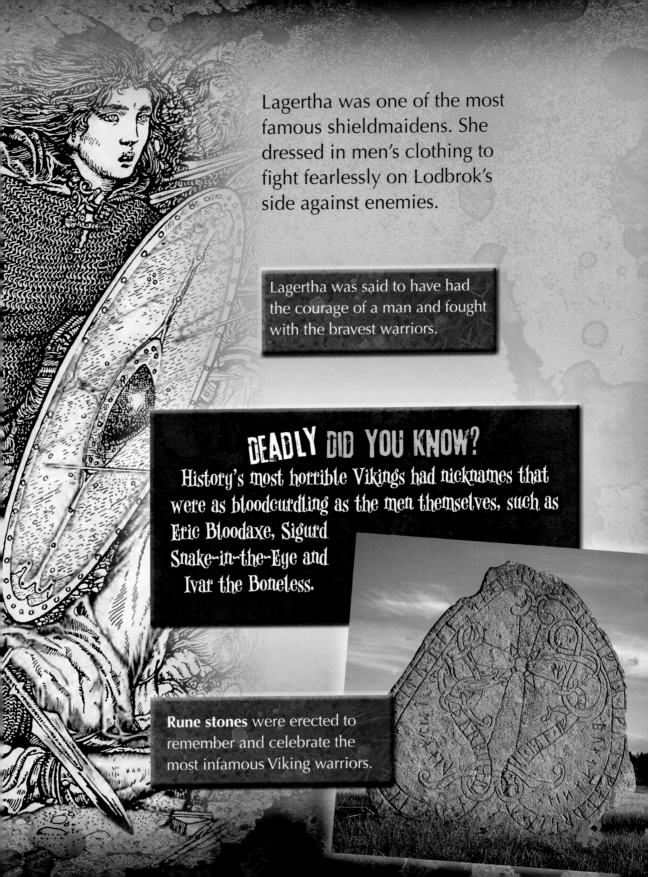

Lagertha was one of the most famous shieldmaidens. She dressed in men's clothing to fight fearlessly on Lodbrok's side against enemies.

Lagertha was said to have had the courage of a man and fought with the bravest warriors.

DEADLY DID YOU KNOW?

History's most horrible Vikings had nicknames that were as bloodcurdling as the men themselves, such as Eric Bloodaxe, Sigurd Snake-in-the-Eye and Ivar the Boneless.

Rune stones were erected to remember and celebrate the most infamous Viking warriors.

Vanquished Vikings

The Vikings were vicious raiders and brutal warriors but their reign of terror could not go on forever. The Vikings were **vanquished** partly in bloody battles, but also by choice.

People had grown tired of the Vikings' reign. They grouped together to defend themselves against Viking attacks. Vikings lost savage fights for control in many countries. The last Viking king of York, Eric Bloodaxe, was expelled from Northumbria in AD 954.

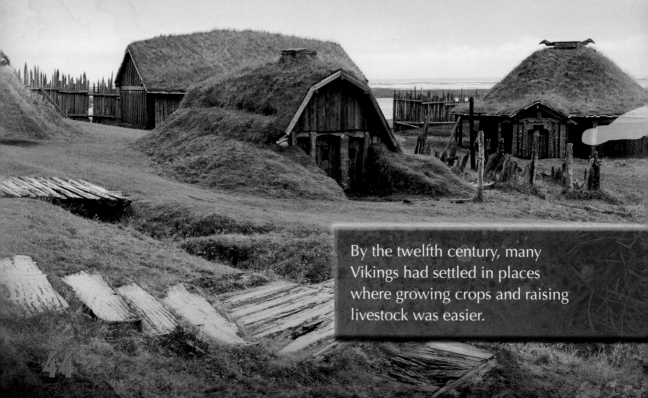

By the twelfth century, many Vikings had settled in places where growing crops and raising livestock was easier.

By the twelfth century, most Vikings had settled down. Many became Christians and forgot their old Viking gods. The age of the mighty and murderous Vikings was over.

KILLER FACT!

The Vikings are famous for being bloodthirsty killers, but there is proof that by the end of the Viking age, many had left behind their murderous ways. Viking rune stones called the Jelling stones have a figure of Jesus Christ on the cross – a sign that the Vikings had become Christians and were no longer seafaring warriors.

The Jelling stones were erected in memory of a king's parents. Rune stones such as this were erected near roads or bridges, so that many people could see them.

Glossary

afterlife life after death. Some people believe that after we die we go to live in another world.

Anglo-Saxon relating to the Germanic inhabitants of England from their arrival in the fifth century AD to the Norman Conquest in 1066

antler horn of a deer

bacteria tiny living things that can help waste to rot

beheaded killed by cutting off the person's head

chain mail armour made of small metal rings linked together

conquer use force to take over a city or country

fermented food that contains bacteria that are good for you

figureheads wooden carvings at the front of a ship

friction force that makes it difficult for things to move freely when they are touching each other

grove group of trees close together

inhabited lived in

inherit receive something from someone who has died

invaders people, armies or countries that use force to enter and take control of another country

lethal deadly

manuscripts handwritten documents

mass grave grave where many bodies are buried together

menacing threatening harm or danger

monastery building or group of buildings where monks live

monks holy men who devote their life to their Christian religion and live with other monks in a monastery

Norse language of ancient Norway, Sweden and Denmark

opponents people fighting against another army or group

plunder steal from a place

rune stones stones with runes, letters from the Viking alphabet, carved into them

sacrifice animal or human killed to honour a god or gods

Scandinavia group of countries that includes Denmark, Norway and Sweden

settlements places where people live and have built homes

slaves people who are owned by other people and have to obey them

vanquished beaten or defeated

Find out more

Books

DKfindout! Vikings, Philip Steele (DK Children, 2018)

Norse Myths and Legends (All About Myths),
Anita Ganeri (Raintree, 2015)

The Viking and Anglo-Saxon Struggle for England
(Early British History), Claire Throp (Raintree, 2016)

The Viking Express (Newspapers from History),
Andrew Langley (Raintree, 2018)

The Vikings (History Hunters), Louise Spilsbury
(Raintree, 2016)

Websites

www.bbc.com/bitesize/articles/zcpf34j
Learn more about the Vikings.

www.dkfindout.com/uk/history/vikings
Find out more about the Vikings and take a quiz to test
your knowledge.

www.jorvikvikingcentre.co.uk
Discover more about the Vikings.

Index